BOYS & GIRLS
COME OUT TO PLAY
and other
nursery rhymes

Illustrated by Carolyn Scrace

CARNIVAL

Mary had a little lamb,
   Its fleece was white as snow;
And everywhere that Mary went
   The lamb was sure to go.

It followed her to school one day,
   That was against the rule;
It made the children laugh and play
   To see a lamb at school.

And so the teacher turned it out,
   But still it lingered near,
And waited patiently about
   Till Mary did appear.

Why does the lamb love Mary so?
   The eager children cry;
Why, Mary loves the lamb, you know,
   The teacher did reply.

Rain, rain, go away,
Come again another day,
Little Johnny wants to play.

Humpty Dumpty sat on a wall,
Humpty Dumpty had a great fall;
All the King's horses
And all the King's men
Couldn't put Humpty together again.

Little Miss Muffet
    Sat on a tuffet,
Eating her curds and whey;
    There came a big spider,
Who sat down beside her
    And frightened Miss Muffet away.

Doctor Foster went to Gloucester
In a shower of rain;
He stepped in a puddle,
Right up to his middle,
And never went there again.

Lavender's blue, diddle, diddle,
Lavender's green;
When I am king, diddle, diddle.
You shall be queen.

Gee up Neddy, to the fair;
What shall we buy when we get there?
A penny apple and a penny pear;
Gee up, Neddy, to the fair.

Jack and Jill
   Went up the hill,
To fetch a pail of water;
   Jack fell down,
And broke his crown,
   And Jill came tumbling after.

Then up Jack got,
   And home did trot,
As fast as he could caper;
   He went to bed
To mend his head
   With vinegar and brown paper.

Little Poll Parrot
　Sat in his garret
Eating toast and tea;
　A little brown mouse
Jumped into the house,
　And stole it all away.

Ding, dong, bell,
Pussy's in the well.
Who put her in?
Little Johnny Green.
Who pulled her out?
Little Tommy Stout.
What a naughty boy was that
To try to drown poor pussy cat,
Who never did him any harm,
And killed the mice in his father's barn.

Teddy Bear, Teddy Bear, turn around,
Teddy Bear, Teddy Bear, touch the ground.

Teddy Bear, Teddy Bear, read the news,
Teddy Bear, Teddy Bear, shine your shoes.

Teddy Bear, Teddy Bear, go upstairs,
Teddy Bear, Teddy Bear, say your prayers.

Teddy Bear, Teddy Bear, turn out the light,
Teddy Bear, Teddy Bear, say GOOD NIGHT!

Hector Protector was dressed all in green;
Hector Protector was sent to the Queen.
The Queen did not like him,
No more did the King;
So Hector Protector was sent back again.

Boys and girls come out to play,
The moon doth shine as bright as day.
Leave your supper and leave your sleep,
And join your playfellows in the street.
Come with a whoop and come with a call,
Come with a good will or not at all.
Up the ladder and down the wall,
A half-penny loaf will serve us all;
You find milk, and I'll find flour,
And we'll have a pudding in half an hour.

Little Jack Sprat
Once had a pig;
It was not very little,
Nor yet very big,
It was not very lean,
It was not very fat —
It's a good pig to grunt,
Said little Jack Sprat.

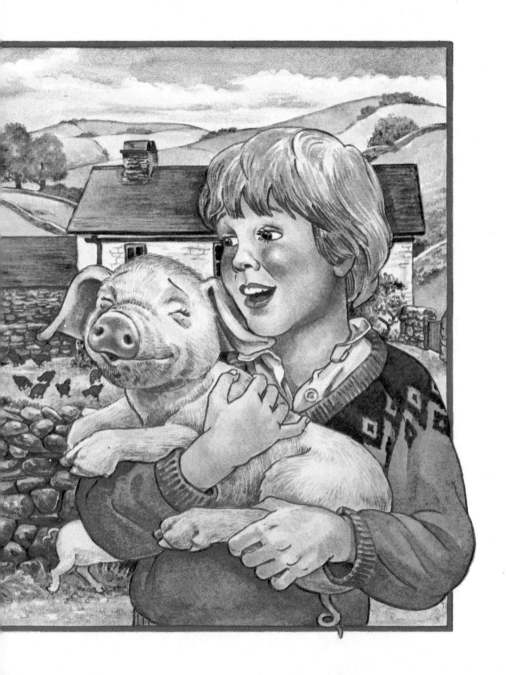

Pit, pat, well-a-day,
Little Robin flew away;
Where can little Robin be?
Gone into the cherry tree.

I'll tell you a story
About Jack-a-Nory,
And now my story's begun;
I'll tell you another
Of Jack and his brother,
And now my story is done.